Matryoshkas in Therapy

Creative ways to use Russian dolls with clients

Christine & Roger Day

Brook Creative Therapy

About the authors

Roger Day

Certified Transactional Analyst, Psychotherapist and Play Therapy specialist

For many years Roger has been a trainer and supervisor specialising in children and families. Now retired, he lives in Rugby, Warwickshire.

Christine Day

European Adult Teaching Certificate, Nursery Nurse Examination Board (NNEB), Diploma in Counselling, Certificate in Counselling Skills

Christine is a qualified nursery nurse. In addition to successfully raising four children, over the years she has added play and creativity specialisms to her nursery skills. Christine lives with Roger in Rugby, Warwickshire.

Books by Roger & Christine Day:
Matryoshkas in Therapy: Creative ways to use Russian dolls with clients
Creative Anger Expression
Creative Therapy in the Sand: Using sandtray with clients

Christine & Roger Day have also published the following books in CD-ROM form:
Body Awareness: 64 bodywork activities for therapy (2008/2011)
Therapeutic Adventure: 64 activities for therapy outdoors (2008/2011)
Stories that Heal: 64 creative visualisations for use in therapy (2011)

Brook Creative Therapy, Brook Cottage, 16 Burnside, Rugby CV22 6AX, UK

4

Acknowledgements

Russian dolls have been around for over 100 years. Yet it is only in recent years that their power in therapeutic work with clients has been recognised. This short book reflects our own development as therapists in this important field.

There have been a number of trainers and supervisors whose creative approaches have given us the inspiration to develop a book on creativity using Matryoshka nesting dolls. We appreciate the input of Joseph Zinker, Bob Davis, Keith Tudor, Monika Jephcott and John Daly, to name but a few.

This book had its origins in two articles we wrote a couple of years ago for the Romanian Association of Transactional Analysis (ARAT) bulletin. They were entitled (in English) *Helping Clients Using Russian Dolls* and *Theory Behind Therapy Using Russian Dolls.*

Above all, we are grateful to the many clients, supervisees and trainees in the UK and Romania who have given feedback on the use of Russian dolls in their sessions. Thank you one and all.

Christine & Roger Day
April 2012

Foreword by Bob Davis

During their recent visit here in Spain, Roger & Christine Day approached me to write the foreword to their new book, *Matryoshkas in Therapy.* I was both pleasantly surprised and, oddly, somewhat shocked.

I have owned a set of Russian dolls for four decades, having purchased them on a trip to Moscow and Leningrad in the early 1970s. But I have never used them in therapy with patients/clients. Those 40 years were clearly part of a *fertile void* for me on the Gestalt cycle!

A book on Matryoshkas in therapy seemed at first a slightly quirky idea. Looking back, I should be a little ashamed of myself. Being a Gestalt trained therapist, how could such as useful therapeutic object sitting on my mantlepiece have escaped my *awareness?* Well, for 40 years, it did.

Roger & Christine's book is both useful practically and an excellent theoretically, creative and integrative stimulant for counsellors, psychotherapists and play therapists.

I have known Roger & Christine for over two decades. I can therefore testify to their competence and skill at working creatively and effectively with clients, both young and old. They are competent therapists, trainers and writers whose work will aid you and excite you.

I enjoyed *Matryoshkas in Therapy* and am *satisfied* (having completed the Gestalt cycle) that I have leaned and gained from two of my past students in such an illuminating way.

Спасибо (spasibo)*, Roger & Christine, and on to the next book, I hope.

Bob Davis MA
Almeria, Spain
April 2012

* Russian for 'thank you'.

Bob Davis is a practicing psychotherapist and trainer. He is a qualified teacher, psychotherapist, social worker and counselling supervisor. He has worked in the NHS and done many years' work with disaffected young people. He can be contacted by email: bdavisjupiter@gmail.com

Background to Matryoshkas

Sometimes what seems like a normal household item can have an amazing effect on clients. Take Russian dolls, for instance. They are popular as ornaments all around the world. As the biggest one is opened, out comes a smaller one, and so on right down to the very smallest doll.

We use a five-doll set specifically for our therapy, training and supervision. (Christine keeps her own set in the house as an ornament, away from any use in therapy.) Every time we use Russian dolls in a therapeutic way, it has a profound effect on the person.

Russian dolls were originally produced in 1890 and known as nesting dolls. Vasily Zvyozdochkin carved the first one, and it was painted by Russian folk crafts painter Sergey Malyutin of Abramtsevo. It consisted of eight dolls, the outer holding a rooster and the innermost a baby, carved in one piece. Its inspiration came from a doll that had come from Honshu, the main island of Japan.

Matryoshkas (or, more correctly, Matryoshki) are traditionally carved from wood that comes from the lime tree (known as linden or basswood in the USA). This wood has been dried for at least two years. A block of wood is cut in half and a piece for each doll is taken from each of the two halves.

The Russian name for them, Matryoshka, means 'little maiden'. It is a diminutive of the female name Matryona. It can also refer to 'mother' and is certainly associated with a healthy, well-built peasant woman heading up her family. You will notice that Russian dolls always look well fed! In Western countries the word 'Baboushka' has often been used when referring to Russian dolls. Baboushka means grandmother in Russian and it is too far from the original name to be used in this book.

The outer doll of a Matryoshka set is usually shown wearing a sarafan. This is a traditional Russian shapeless jumper-dress (pinafore), which is now worn mainly for folk singing and dancing.

Certain parts of Russia have come to be associated with the manufacture of Matryoshkas. Sergiyev Posad in Moscow's suburbs is particularly famous for Russian dolls. It is, coincidentally, also well known for Holy Trinity-St Sergius Lavra, the monastry founded by St Sergius of Radonezeh in 1337.

In 1922 a family business was started in the town of Semenov, near Nizhny Novgorod, to make Russian dolls. Ten years later the business was expanded to include other families. Semenov Russian dolls are distinctive for their floral patterns, the inclusion of an apron, the use of aniline dyes, space that has not been decorated, and the use of varnish.

The largest Matryoshkas, one metre high and consisting of 72 pieces, were made in Semenov.

In recent years Russian doll manufacture has been in decline. Other countries, including Bulgaria and China, have taken up the task. Chinese Matryoshkas in particular are often mass-produced and lacking distinction from each other.

How to choose the right set for you

There are many different styles of Russian dolls. When you are buying a set choose a style that suits you and your clients.

You might consider a set with traditional floral patterns based on the Semenov style (see page 9). You could choose one from the pastoral genre, with the patterns burned on using pyrography (wood burning using a tool with a special heated tip). Other patterns you might prefer may be based on fairy stories or animals.

Many Russian dolls have a religious theme involving icon-type figures or Christian special occasions such as Easter and Christmas. While these may be very appealing as ornaments, we wonder whether the themes could limit their use with clients. The same would apply to specific themes such as Russian leaders when, during the 1980s, *perestroika* (restructuring) was the popular political term, or more recently the characters from the Harry Potter film series.

What happens if you work with a male client? After all, most Matryoshkas – at least the outer ones – are based on an adult female. While it is possible to find men and boys within sets of Russian dolls (the original set had a small boy among the eight dolls), it is rare to get hold of a fully male set.

Our experience is that most male clients will happily work with a traditional set, applying their own gender to them even if the dolls have distinctive feminine features and clothing. In some cases, men may use the dolls to explore their more tender attributes along the lines of poet Carl Sandburg's (1878-1967) describing Abraham Lincoln as a man of both steel *and velvet.*

We recommend a set with between four and 12 dolls, getting smaller and smaller. Ensure that the dolls can be pulled apart and handled easily. They do not have to be new or even attractive. They may have appeal to clients because they have chipped paint or faded facial features.

Spend time looking at the face of each doll before you buy. The outside one usually has a big smile but as they get smaller the smile often turns into a surprised, sad or scared expression. Look especially at the very smallest one. With the set we use in therapy, each doll has a different expression. Our set has a tiny doll with a very sad face that is ideal for helping clients to explore early childhood trauma. Of course, each client will use intuition to apply to the dolls certain emotions and thinking. Having different facial expressions, though, could help in that process.

Finally, once you have chosen your Matryoshka set, whether new or secondhand, make sure that it is well cared for. Keep it away from sand, water and direct sunlight. If a piece is accidentally broken, that doesn't mean the whole set is useless. Our advice is to fix the broken piece as best you can (wood glue works well) and keep using the set in therapy. If the halves become difficult to separate, try applying a small amount of furniture polish or wax to the joints. If all else fails, use sandpaper or a small file to help the pieces open and close more easily.

Theory behind Russian dolls

There are several theoretical ways to understand what is happening when the person opens and reflects on each doll in a set of Russian dolls. Here are a few ideas for consideration. There are more within the activities themselves.

Child ego state

According to Transactional Analysis there are three different ways of being in the world. These ways of being are known as Parent, Adult and Child ego states. Eric Berne defined an ego state as 'a consistent pattern of feeling and experience, directly related to a corresponding consistent pattern of behaviour' (Berne, 1966/94, page 364).

Stewart & Joines (1987) described them as follows:

Parent ego state: 'A set of behaviours, thoughts and feelings which have been copied from parents or parent-figures' (page 331).

Adult ego state: 'A set of behaviours, thoughts and feelings which are direct responses to the here-and-now, not copied from parents or parent-figures nor replayed from the individual's own childhood' (page 326).

Child ego state: 'A set of behaviours, thoughts and feelings which are replayed from the individual's own childhood' (page 327).

As each doll is revealed, the person could be seen as working with the Child ego state at different ages and stages of development. The person talking about a particular doll could, for instance, see his or her six-year-old Child as stuck or limited by the situations around. Or the Child could be seen as resourceful in finding creative ways to cope with the chaos around him or her.

Hargaden & Sills (2003) write: 'The striving of the child for the perfect sense of attunement and loving attachment that may have eluded his infanthood, or been too early abrupted in childhood, acts as a positive symbol for change' (page 191).

Deconfusion
Another way to work with the Child ego state is to encourage the person holding the doll to do deconfusion work with his or her own Child ego state at a particular age. This is achieved through the person – assisted by the therapist – engaging in a transferential relationship with their own Child as symbolised in the doll. This involves four steps: developing an empathic relationship; engaging in a transferential relationship; examining countertransference; and responding to the client (the person's own Child ego state). For more on this see Hargaden & Sills, 1999, page 20.

Inner Child
Using the Child ego state in these ways has parallels with John Bradshaw's Inner Child model of therapy. Bradshaw takes the view that when the Inner Child is wounded this contaminates intimacy in relationships and the child loses his or her sense of self. He writes: 'When a parent cannot affirm his child's feelings, needs and desires, he rejects that child's authentic self. Then a false self must be set up' (Bradshaw, 1990, page 18).

Working with Russian dolls the client can go through various ages and stages to find not just the negatives but the positive coping mechanisms in the child that was the client's self at a particular age. Bradshaw's goal is to help the client become a hero to that particular Inner Child.

He writes: 'There is surely rejoicing when we reclaim and champion our wounded inner child. For many of us, finding our inner child is like finding home for the first time' (Bradshaw, 1990, page 286).

Rubberbands
A rubberband occurs when a person responds to a difficult current situation by snapping back to an 'old, familiar,

childhood feeling, which is being expressed *here and now'* (Kupper & Haimowitz, 1971, page 10). In a sense, by choosing the age of each doll, the person using the Russian dolls is snapping back to those ages foremost in his or her thinking and feeling, where significant events happened.

Erskine (1974) proposed ways to disconnect rubberbands:

'Re-experiencing past feelings which are the same as current ones;

Receiving Permission and Protection to feel and express those feelings which are not expressed in the original situation;

Taking control of the situation and owning the related not-OK decisions;

Recognising how early decisions have and are still affecting life; . . .

Making a new OK decision' (page 119).

Senses of the self

Daniel Stern, in his theory of child development, talks about the child's 'senses of self': emergent self; core self; subjective self; verbal self (see Stern, 1985). Unlike most other child development theories, in Stern's 'senses of self' the person can return to earlier stages to get what he or she missed the first time round.

Using a Russian doll can help to move between the 'senses of self' so the person can work towards healing.

Working with clients using Matryoshkas

When you are working with clients using Matryoshkas it is important to be aware of how the work is affecting your client. Here are some points to be aware of:

Facial expression

While the client is using the Matryoshkas focus on his or her face and not the hands. This takes some practice because the natural tendency is to look at what the hands are doing. Position yourself so your main focus is on the client's face and yet you can still see the dolls out of the corner of your eye. What do you observe? Look for tiny movements around the eyes and in the forehead. Use your own intuition to consider the significance of those movements.

Attitude towards the dolls

How does the client hold the Russian dolls? Does he or she hold them gently, stroking them? Or is the client rough and uncaring, even dismissive?

Tone of voice

Listen to the client's tone of voice. Is the voice quiet, indicating introspection? Angry? Aggressive? Timid? Intimidated? Perhaps the client changes his or her voice to that of a small child?

Postures and gestures

How is the client sitting? Relaxed and reasonably still? Tense? Leaning forward? Hunched up? Arms folded in a protective manner? Legs tense? Or relaxed? Feet still? Or tapping? Legs tightly crossed? Leg swinging? Fiddling with hair? Stroking an imaginary beard?

Breathing

Can you hear the client breathing? Is the client holding his or her breath? Breathing fast and shallow? Or deeply? Is the client sighing? Or making sounds that are not words?

One way to work out what is happening within a person while using Matryoshkas is to consider an ego state diagnosis based on behavioural clues. This involves using observation of tiny changes in face, voice and body position that are closely linked to Eric Berne's original work on intuition. There are five key elements here:

❏ Words
❏ Tones
❏ Gestures
❏ Postures
❏ Facial expressions

For more on this see Stewart & Joines, 1987, chapter 5).

Things to remember

Your camera

Remember to photograph what the client creates using the Matryoshkas. You might need to take several pictures to show the changes the client has made.

Photographs are important for your own notekeeping and also for your client, if he or she would like them.

Remember, too, that if you store on a computer any photographs or other personal information about your clients you are required in the UK to register with the Information Commissioner's Office. This currently costs £35 per year. Further details are available from: www.ico.gov.uk

A box of tissues

Using Matryoshkas in therapy can lead to surprising and very powerful results.

We always like to have tissues available for these exercises. This gives a nonverbal permission for the person to cry if they want to. At the same time, they don't have to cry!

We invite the person to hold the dolls and talk in the third person ('he' or 'she') because it is more comfortable and less threatening during what for many clients are very powerful exercises.

Layers of life

One way of using Russian dolls in therapy is what we call 'Layers of life'.

First, hand the person the complete set of dolls fixed together. Here is how we usually explain it to the person. Remember to vary the questions and use 'he' if working with a man. Above all, use intuition and follow the client's lead.

This is a Russian doll. It has lots of layers. It's a bit like us because we are made up of the same person at different ages. So inside you there is a six-year-old and a three-year-old as well as the age you are right now. All of life's experiences so far have made you the person you are today – both bad things and good things.

OK, have a look at the Russian doll and tell me about her right now. What kind of person is she?

Now open up the first layer and look at the second doll. Without thinking too hard, what is the age of this doll? What is she like? How does she feel? What is she thinking?

Now the third doll. What is the first age that comes to your head? What is she like? What happened to her at that age? Does she feel safe? What does she think about the world around her?

Now open up to the fourth doll. What age is she? What is she like as a person? What is happening to her at that age?

Finally, open up and look at the smallest doll. What age is she? What is she like? How does she feel? Is she welcomed by her family? How loved does she feel?

This is the other person's work. The therapist is there to empower, support and encourage.

This activity can be used over several sessions. It doesn't need to be completed in one discussion.

It is useful to encourage the person to feel empathy towards each of the dolls. It is important that he or she takes time and does not rush through traumatic episodes. Our aim is to help the person acknowledge the pain and connect with the doll, understanding the real – possibly unexpressed – needs of the child at each age and stage. You may find that the person needs to express in the present the feelings and needs that are being spoken about.

Using Russian dolls in this way can enable a person to reconnect with the child they once were and celebrate the courage of that child in finding ways to survive.

Making changes

Introduce the Matryoshkas to your client. Explain that the set is composed of smaller dolls who, because of life experiences, have made up the present (largest) doll.

Invite your client to open up and explore the set of Russian dolls and set them out on a flat surface.

Discuss with your client the fact that things happen to us that mould and shape our characters. Many things may have occurred at different times for these dolls, and together those things make up the person she is today.

Encourage your client to talk about some of these things that have happened to the smaller dolls and how they have affected the largest doll.

Ask your client what changes he or she would like to make with the largest doll. Remind your client that the past cannot be changed. What *can* be changed is how the doll deals with situations now and in the future.

Discuss practically how these changes can be made and how they will affect the doll.

As with other activities, be ready to use this activity over several sessions, even returning to it after a time.

Who is the real me?

Matryoshkas are ideal to help clients with identity issues. Through them clients can answer the question: 'Who is the real me?'

Invite your client to hold the largest of the Russian dolls containing all the other dolls. After some moments invite the client to put them all out on a flat surface.

Ask: 'Which doll is you right now?' Then invite the client to hold that particular doll.

Next begin to explore with the client about identity by asking questions or giving prompts: 'Tell me about her.' 'What is she like?' 'What does she enjoy doing?' 'Is she happy or sad?' 'Is she content or angry?'

You might then ask: 'Is she happy being the way she is? Or is she like this because that's the way other people expect her to be?'

Finally, ask: 'Who does she want to be?' Encourage your client to explore this in depth and to consider what steps have to be taken to achieve this goal.

This activity involving Russian dolls can be used to help confront any negative messages that have been passed down to a client from a family or cultural script. Clients often come to therapy with beliefs about themselves based on other people's expectations. Pearl Drago (1983) identified these expectations as part of a person's Cultural Parent. The Cultural Parent directs the behaviour of the individual. It is based on beliefs and attitudes that have been swallowed whole from family and other cultural scripts.

Trainer Rosemary Napper (2009) explains this by telling the story of five monkeys in a cage. This story could be used with your client to help him or her understand cultural script.

There is a banana on a string above a set of steps. One of the monkeys starts to climb up to get the banana. As soon as he touches the first step all the other monkeys are sprayed with cold water.

Another tries and the same thing happens. Soon the monkeys try to stop anyone wanting to use the steps.

The cold water is put away and one monkey is replaced. The new monkey sees the banana and heads for the steps. He is surprised when he is attacked by the others. As each of the original monkeys is replaced one by one, all the others attack him if he tries to get the banana.

None of the original monkeys has ever been sprayed with cold water, but they all avoid the banana. None of them knows why. As far as they know that is the way it has always been done. The monkeys have developed a well-hidden cultural script.

Matryoshkas and permissions

Matryoshkas can help people claim for themselves in the here and now permissions that they did not receive as children.

Psychotherapists Bob and Mary Goulding identified 12 types of negative decisions made in early childhood that they named 'injunctions' (Goulding & Goulding, 1976). These include Don't Think, Don't Grow Up and Don't Enjoy. Some of these 'Don't' messages are passed on to each of us, usually nonverbally, by parents and other significant adults.

Each injunction has an opposite known as a permission. Stewart & Joines (1987) point out that 'Don't' messages convey a blanket prohibition while permissions are usually preceded by 'It's OK to', which invites the person to decide whether to do something or not.

The 12 permissions are as follows. It's OK to:

Exist	Be yourself	Be a child
Grow up	Make it	Be important
Be close	Belong	Be well
Be sane	Think	Feel

Invite your client to open up and spread out the Russian dolls. From the above list suggest that your client choose a permission for each of the dolls. This is best done intuitively without thinking too much about each permission. It is likely then that the client will already be carrying elements of the injunction that is the opposite to the permission.

The client then holds each doll in turn. Together explore what that permission is likely to look like, sound like and feel like. Invite your client to describe the doll as if he/she already has that permission. Celebrate the success of the doll in accepting that permission before moving on to the next one.

As your client continues to explore and celebrate permissions in the Russian dolls it is hoped that the permissions will also be taken by the client.

This activity could take several sessions. In order to remember what the client's work has been, invite the client to make little labels showing the permissions to put in front of the relevant Russian dolls. Then take a photograph so that you have a record of what was decided at the beginning of this exercise.

It may also be empowering to print a copy of the picture for the client to take home. This will remind the client of the permissions being taken.

Care for self

It is important that clients care for themselves. This care for self extends to care for the 'little client' at different ages and stages as well as the client in the here and now.

Look together at the Matryoshkas and invite your client to set them up on a flat surface.

You as the therapist explain to your client that the dolls are all part of the same person. They represent different ages and stages of life, coming together to make a whole person.

Invite the client to look at the dolls individually and tell you about each of them.

How old are they?

Are they happy to be that age?

Are they carefree? Or troubled?

Are they extrovert? Or introvert?

Do they feel safe? Or unsafe?

Are they loved? Or unloved?

Once some basic information about each doll has been explored, invite the client to look at self care. How can each doll care for herself/himself at the different ages represented? What more is needed to provide the protection the dolls need at the different stages?

This exercise helps clients to build confidence and self-esteem. It is useful especially when a client is bullied at work, college or school.

Relating in the workplace

Pass the Matryoshka to your client and invite him (or her) to arrange the dolls to show the different people at work.

Suggest that the client place the doll representing himself on the surface and move it to show how the doll relates to the other dolls at work.

Discuss the scene in front of you. Ask the client if he is happy with what he has portrayed. How are the dolls arranged? Is the client's doll on the edge? Close to people? Far away? Or overwhelmed?

Suggest that the client tells you what happens in these relationships. Celebrate the good things. How can the client change the things he is not happy with?

Try different scenarios. Ask:

'How would it feel if your doll was a vital part of the team?'

'What would it look like if things were going well?'

'Where would the dolls be positioned in an ideal world?'

'How would this be achieved?'

Be patient. It may take several sessions before the client is able to make the changes he desires. Remember to take photographs at each stage.

Senses of self

Matryoshkas can be used when a client needs to go through his or her own development as a child to explore areas that may be deficient or need further work in therapy.

Pam Levin-Landheer (1982) believes there are seven stages in the 'cycle of development':

Being (0 to 6 months) – the child wants to be physically close and develop a loving, sensual and intensely emotional bond with another person.

Doing (6 to 18 months) – the period of exploring the world around.

Thinking (18 months to 3 years) – the stage of learning independence.

Identity (3 to 6 years) – social relationships, separating fantasy from reality.

Being skilful (6 to 12 years) – discovering tools, skills and values.

Regeneration (13 to 18 years) – discovering sexuality, a personal view on life, a place in the grown-up world.

Recycling (19 years plus) – developing and maintaining relationships, going back and unsticking areas that have been stuck in the person's life.

Choose the number of stages to explore according to the number of dolls in the set. Then with your client begin exploring each stage and what it means to the client. For instance, a client whose parents were neglectful in the first months of life may need to revisit the 'Being' stage and learn

33

to *be* instead of just to *do*. He or she may need to find time to rest, enjoy and engage in positive self-nurture. This is not a process to rush. It may take several sessions.

Daniel Stern's developmental model (Stern, 1985), on the other hand, takes the view that each 'sense of self' and 'domain of relatedness' (towards others) is built on the foundation of the previous one. Stern writes: 'Once formed, the domains remain for ever as distinct forms of experiencing social life and self. None are lost to adult experience. Each simply gets more elaborated' (Stern, 1985, page 32).

Using the Russian dolls with this model, ensure there are four dolls to represent the senses of self – emergent (0-2 months), core (starting at 2-3 months), subjective (from 7-9 months) and verbal (from about 15 months). The same can be used for domains of relatedness – emergent, then core, then intersubjective, then verbal. You might invite your client to use the Russian dolls by starting with the smallest (emergent) and building up the senses of self and domains of relatedness towards other people.

This relational approach to child development helps the client to see how relating at these early stages of life can influence how he or she relates in the here and now.

Discovering the inner child

Russian dolls can be used effectively to help clients 'reclaim and champion [their] wounded inner child' (Bradshaw, 1990, page 286).

Present the set of Matryoshkas to the client. Say something like: 'This Russian doll represents you, probably where you are now. Inside are aspects of you at different ages and stages. This is sometimes known as the inner child.

'Now, I invite you to open them all up and set them down on a flat surface.

'Look at each one and tell me about him or her. Think about the doll's age. Hopes and dreams. Difficulties and strengths. Triumphs and tragedies.

'What is happening in his/her life at this age?'

Encourage your client to look at the individual Russian dolls in terms of heroes who made the best decisions they could make at the various times. Explore the strengths of each doll.

Then, with the client, celebrate the inner child who survived to make your client the stronger person he or she is today.

Finding a support system

Russian dolls can be used to help clients explore their own support system.

Clients are invited to set up the dolls on a surface to represent the support system they currently have in their lives. This support system could include family, friends and work colleagues. It could include you as their therapist. Support could also cover their home and possessions and clients' own abilities, qualifications and personal qualities. Clients might need prompting or may prefer to work in silence.

Once they have finished this stage, invite them to tell you about what they have created.

Things that you could then discuss together include:

❏ Whether or not the client has included a doll to represent himself/herself. If so, what kind of doll is it, and what size?
❏ The other dolls' position and their relative size. Is their a significance in the sizes or are they all of equal importance?

Look together with your clients at the support system they have in place. Is it adequate? Or does it need strengthening? What changes are needed to ensure that the support system is adequate? Invite them to make those changes.

Finally, look together at your clients' support system and celebrate it together.

Working with the family

Individual clients can explore their current family or family of origin using the Matryoshkas.

Clients are invited to unpack the Russian dolls and spread them out on a surface in front of them to represent the family.

Ask them to tell you about the family members in front of you both. Who are they? What are they like? What sort of personalities do they have? Which one is the client? Observe and comment on the the size of this Matryoshka in relation to the other family members.

Invite clients if they have not already done so to arrange the Russian dolls so that they are connected as in the family. This might take some time and the client may need to work uninterrupted.

Look together at what clients have created. What do you both see? Is that how they thought their family would look like? Or did they expect it to look completely different?

What impact does the family portrayed here have on the clients? If you work relationally, consider your own internal processes when looking at the family and, if appropriate, share these with your clients.

Ask what your clients would like to change about the family, bearing in mind that it is impossible to change other people. Then invite them to make those changes. Again, give plenty of space and time for clients to make the changes necessary.

Look at the family again. Is your client happy with this? Or is another change needed? Carry on inviting small changes until clients are happy.

This may take several sessions. With this in mind, photograph each scene so that clients can set it all up in the same way at the next appointment.

Social masks

Matryoshkas can be used as a form of social mask.

Introduce the client to the Russian dolls. Explain that the largest doll can be seen as a mask. Ask your client: 'Is the mask how you want the world to see you? Or is it how the world expects you to be, and you're conforming to that expectation?'

Invite the client to start opening the Russian dolls and thus start taking off the mask. What is inside? Which of the smaller dolls is the real person? (It may be more than one.)

Explore with the client how the doll feels without the mask. How is she going to protect herself? Is it safe, or does she need to put the mask back on again?

It is important that the therapist is aware of the client's need for protection. The doll may have to wear the mask in public or in certain situations. The doll needs to feel safe, with strong boundaries. Explore with the client when it could be safe not to have the mask on.

Therapist, remember that at some point this mask was essential for her protection, even for life itself (such as in cases of child abuse). The mask may no longer be useful but it has become a part of the client's armoury.

This is a major script change and will not happen lightly. Be prepared to give this exercise time, maybe touching on it and coming back after several sessions to look at it again. Remember to take a photograph for your records and for the client to look at afresh.

The experiment

Matryoshkas can be used for creative experiments when both therapist and client seem 'stuck' in the therapy.

Such stuck places could be seen in a negative way. Or they could be viewed as a vital part of the therapeutic process. For instance, the Gestalt cycle of experience involves moving into and away from 'full and vibrant contact'. In between two cycles of experience within therapy there is the resting position, known as the fertile void, in which anything can happen. This is the point when an experiment involving Russian dolls can be highly effective.

Gestalt therapy emphasises modifying a client's behaviour in the therapy situation itself. When such 'systematic behaviour modification' grows out of the client's experience, is called an experiment.

Gestalt psychotherapist Joseph Zinker explains: 'The experiment is the cornerstone of experiential learning. It transforms talking about into doing, stale reminiscing and theorising into being fully here with all one's imagination, energy and excitement. For example, by acting out an old, unfinished situation, the client is able to comprehend it in its richest context and to complete the experience using the resources of his present wisdom and understanding of life' (Zinker, 1977, page 123).

An experiment using Russian dolls is first contracted with the client. You as the therapist might propose the experiment based on your own intuition. Or the client might want to use the Russian dolls to deal with an issue but doesn't know how to go about it. Part of the contract is to agree together that the experiment, by its very definition, might or might not work. Once the contract is established, the client may look at the dolls and decide what to do with them (bearing in mind that they break easily). Or you as the therapist may propose lining them up or putting one in each corner of the therapy room, with the fifth one in the middle.

What happens next? Again, it is important to go with the flow of an experiment, tapping into your own intuition and inviting your client to tap into his or hers. You might suggest that the client imagines being each of the dolls in turn and talking about what he or she sees and hears from that position. This can be done in the here and now. The client may decide to move the dolls in relation to each other or put one inside a larger one.

Zinker again: 'This process transforms dreams, fantasies, memories, reminiscences and hopes into lively, ongoing, dynamic happenings between therapist and client' (Zinker, 1977, page 124). As you and you client engage with Matryoshka dolls in an experimental way, exciting outcomes are possible. Enjoy together the fertile void!

A positive future

Matryoshkas can be used to help clients move towards a positive outcome or a bright future.

The client's past, present and future can be constructed using the various sizes of Russian dolls. The client may like to spread these out, with the past on the left, the present in the middle and the future on the right. This forms a visual representation of what could be called a timeline. The timeline has been defined as 'the way we store pictures, sounds and feelings of our past, present and future' (O'Connor & Seymour, 1990, page 246).

Neuro-Linguistic Programming (NLP) uses the timeline to help clients move towards a positive future. 'Timelines are important in therapy. If a client cannot see a future for himself, a lot of techniques are not going to work. Many NLP therapy techniques presuppose an ability to move through time, accessing past resources or constructing compelling futures. Sometimes the timeline has to be sorted out before this can be done' (O'Connor & Seymour, 1990, page 137).

Looking at the Russian dolls the client and therapist can decide together how to move the dolls around so that they represent a shift towards a positive future. This does not automatically mean that the largest Russian doll is the 'best' for the future. Indeed, a client with issues around body weight and dieting may find the idea of increasing in size and girth, even only figuratively, strange or even insulting. Rather, it is the client's perception that matters here.

Once the new order is chosen, the therapy can be geared towards achieving the result that has been portrayed visually through the Russian dolls.

This approach with a positive future in view using Matryoshkas could also be used in establishing a contract for change. A contract is an 'explicit bilateral commitment to a well-defined course of action; an Adult commitment to oneself and/or someone else to make a change' (Stewart & Joines, 1987, page 328).

The way a mere wish by a client can be transformed into a contract for change is by the therapist and client agreeing their parts in achieving the goal.

According to Ian Stewart (1996) a therapeutic contract has the following elements:

❏ It is based on actions.
❏ It is sensory based (the result can be seen, heard etc).
❏ It is finishable.

The contract is put in positive terms and is agreed between client and therapist based on the positions of the Russian dolls. A photograph of the final position of the dolls can serve as a reminder of the direction and purpose of the therapy.

Understanding who we are

A set of Matryoshkas can be used to help clients to explore aspects of themselves in the form of what psychologist Carl Jung (Jung, 1964) called archetypes.

Archetypes are themes, or patterns of thinking and behaving, that appear across people, cultures and societies throughout the world. Most people have within themselves several of these themes. Each of the dolls can be used to represent a different archetype, and clients can explore the significance and importance of that archetype in their lives.

Here are some of the main archetypes:

Shadow – dark, chaotic, disturbing yet fascinating.
Anima – feminine image in the man's psyche, soul or true self, leading to the collective unconscious.
Animus – masculine image in the woman's psyche.
Self – the spirit that connects the individual to God; the regulating centre of the psyche.
Persona – the image we present to the world, usually acting as a mask for the ego.
Mother – creative, loving, nurturing and soothing but also destructive and ambivalent.
Father – stern, protective, powerful, controlling.
Trickster – mysterious, hidden.
Hero – rescuer, champion.

Encourage clients to choose from this list an archetype for each doll in the set. Then see how that archetype relates to and affects the client. Finally, look at the dolls chosen. Explore together the significance, if any, of the relative sizes of the dolls in relation to the chosen archetypes represented.

References

Berne, Eric (1994). *Principles of Group Treatment.* Menlo Park, California: Shea Books. (Original work published 1966).

Bradshaw, John (1990). *Homecoming: Reclaiming and championing your inner child.* London: Bantam Books.

Drago, Pearl (1983). The Cultural Parent. *Transactional Analysis Journal, 35,* 4, pages 224-227.

Erskine, Richard (1974). Therapeutic intervention: Disconnecting rubberbands. *Transactional Analysis Journal, 4,* 1, pages 119-120.

Goulding, Bob, & Goulding, Mary (1976). Injunctions, decisions and redecisions. *Transactional Analysis Journal, 6,* 1, pages 41-48.

Hargaden, Helena, & Sills, Charlotte (1999). The Child ego state: An integrative view. *ITA News, 53,* Spring 1999.

Hargaden, Helena, & Sills, Charlotte (2003). 'Who am I for you?': The Child ego state and transferential domains, in Sills, C, & Hargaden, H (eds) (2003). *Ego States.* London: Worth Publishing, pages 185-200.

Jung, Carl G (1964). *Man and His Symbols,* New York: Doubleday.

Kupper, David, & Haimowitz, Morris (1971). Therapeutic interventions: Part 1 – Rubberbands now. *Transactional Analysis Journal, 1,* 1, pages 10-16.

Levin-Landheer, Pam (1982). The cycle of development. *Transactional Analysis Journal, 12,* 2, pages 129-139.

Napper, Rosemary (2009). Personal communication.

O'Connor, Joseph, & Seymour, John (1990). *Introducting Neuro-Lingustic Programming.* London: Aquarian/Thorsons.

Stern, Daniel (1985). *The Interpersonal World of the Infant: A view from psychoanalysis and developmental psychology.* New York: Basic Books.

Stewart, Ian (1996). *Developing Transactional Analysis Counselling.*London: Sage.

Stewart, Ian, & Joines, Vann (1987). *TA Today: A new introduction to transactional analysis.* Nottingham: Lifespace Publishing.

Zinker, Joseph (1977). *Creative Processes in Gestalt Therapy.* New York: Vintage Books.